Aylesbury

in old picture postcards

by
Ralph May

European Library - Zaltbommel/Netherlands MCMLXXXV

GB   ISBN 90 288 3134 7 / CIP

European Library in Zaltbommel/Netherlands publishes among other things the following series:

IN OLD PICTURE POSTCARDS *is a series of books which sets out to show what a particular place looked like and what life was like in Victorian and Edwardian times. A book about virtually every town in the United Kingdom is to be published in this series. By the end of this year about 175 different volumes will have appeared. 1,250 books have already been published devoted to the Netherlands with the title* **In oude ansichten.** *In Germany, Austria and Switzerland 500, 60 and 15 books have been published as* **In alten Ansichten;** *in France by the name* **En cartes postales anciennes** *and in Belgium as* **En cartes postales anciennes** *and/or* **In oude prentkaarten** *150 respectively 400 volumes have been published.*

For further particulars about published or forthcoming books, apply to your bookseller or direct to the publisher.

This edition has been printed and bound by Grafisch Bedrijf De Steigerpoort in Zaltbommel/Netherlands.

INTRODUCTION

God gave all men all earth to love,
But since our hearts are small,
Ordained for each one spot should prove
Belovèd over all.

So wrote Rudyard Kipling in his poem 'Sussex'. For most people this becomes their place of birth probably because the happy memories of childhood gild the scene. In the case of Aylesbury, as I talk to people I find their memories strongly tinged with nostalgia, and regret for the passing of the old town. It had survived comparatively unaltered until the early sixties when the destruction proceeded at great pace, whole streets being demolished, unfortunately largely in the town centre therefore including many of the older properties. They prefer to remember Aylesbury as a busy market town where everybody knew everybody else, and there was time to stop and talk in the streets and markets.

Wednesday and Saturday were market days and brought a great influx of shoppers from the surrounding villages, there was an almost gala atmosphere then. Each village had its own carrier. There would be one, if not two carriers' carts making the journey to town, some daily, others on market days. They came with passengers only and returned with the villagers loaded with a week's shopping, and deliveries from local firms to make on their behalf. Each carrier put up at a given inn or public house for the day, and according to the destination everybody knew where

to find the particular carrier required. Farmers of course had their own transport but for places not on the railway line the carrier was the only means of access. Sheep and cattle were driven to market and the drovers beguiled the day in the local hostelries. The market square was entirely filled from top to bottom with stalls of every description. Many were local traders but others, from as far afield as London, attended regularly. The shopkeepers did not always appreciate the competition but when the market was removed soon realised that it had brought trade rather than harmed them.

I have dealt with the shops in some detail as these were very much part of the town life. Many had been so long established that they served generations of customers most of whom were known personally, and trading was between trusted supplier and valued clients. Family and local news was exchanged making shopping more pleasurable then than now.

Standing at the junction of six main roads, Aylesbury must always have been a busy and thriving town with a constant flow of horse traffic passing through. One has only to realise that for the past four centuries the market square alone was surrounded by seven large inns: The King's Head, the George, the Black Swan, the Crown, the Bull's Head, the White Hart and the Bell. All were extensive properties with courtyards, stabling and ample accommodation for waggons and other vehicles. Many had gardens and pleasure grounds and even bowling greens. All had high double gates to protect the waggon-loads of goods standing overnight. For all these, as well as the six taverns of the same period, to survive and prosper, century after century, tells its own story of a flourishing, crowded market town.

The canal branch came in 1814 taking much of the heavy traffic from the roads. It soon became a busy waterway with barges continually unloading and loading at the wharves in Walton Street; the basin was a scene of constant activity. A small chapel-cum-school was erected by the tow-path for the bargees and their children. It survived until the early twenties. For thirty years the traffic continued to grow and the canal flourished until the coming of the railways.

As soon as the London and North Western Line to Birmingham was established, a branch line was laid to Aylesbury, first for goods — to the yard in Station Street, and then for passengers — to a station opened 10th June 1839 in Railway Street. This was later enlarged, with access to High Street. 1863 saw the opening of the railway station in Great Western Street, a branch line to Princes Risborough having been laid to connect with the Great Western, London to Oxford rail. The Metropolitan and Great Central lines from Baker Street and Marylebone came with the extension of the line from Harrow to Aylesbury. It then became known as the Aylesbury Joint Station.

Up until the industrial development of the town in the 1870's Aylesbury was the centre of a thriving agricultural community based on the rich pastures of the Vale of Aylesbury, hence its busy cattle and sheep markets. The first factories to come were the Anglo-Swiss Condensed Milk Company and Hazell, Watson & Viney, printers and bookbinders, who developed and extended rapidly to become the largest employers in the town. Hunt Barnard and Company, another printing firm, came in 1898 and Aylesbury soon became a printing town.

This book is intended to feature Aylesbury as shown in the postcards of 1880 to 1930. I do not dwell on the introduction and development of the postcard as this is already fully covered in publications and catalogues issued for collectors. All I wish to say is that they form a valuable record of the buildings, places and street scenes of the period, which might well have gone unrecorded otherwise. My own memory of the locality extends over a period of seventy years, and much of what is written is from personal recollection. I have sought to make this book a ready reference which will recall forgotten memories, perhaps help to settle many arguments, and I hope to bring to life again a time and place of fond memory. If it gives a few hours of pleasant reading and subject for conversation I have not wasted my time. A few old original photographs are reproduced, and earlier history is only included where further information was considered necessary. Much of interest has had to be omitted as it lies outside the scope of this book.

1. Church Street, looking towards St Mary's Church from Temple Square. Most of the buildings are 15th and 16th century, but with later façades. It could well be termed Aylesbury's 'Harley Street', as it has for the past 150 years been largely occupied by the medical profession. Number 1 in the right foreground was the home of Dr T.G. Parrott from 1891 to 1951, one of the best loved and most highly respected doctors ever to practice in the town. The house with bay windows was Dr West's, and the building between was shared as surgeries. The upper right side is better shown in card 3. The left foreground house was occupied at the period of the Great War by Captain Nicholls, the officer in command of the Oxford and Bucks Light Infantry. They had their headquarters in the adjoining offices in Temple Square. The remaining buildings up to the Chantry were all part of the infantry headquarters and the Drill Hall. The site is now Lincoln House, the only change in the street.

Church Street, Aylesbury.

2. Continuing on the right side we come to Ceely House, a 15th century building refronted in the early 18th century. The fine porch is worth noting. The façade is covered by a Virginia Creeper at least seventy years old, which in its autumn colours is a joy to behold. The house is named after the Ceely brothers, both early surgeons associated with the Bucks Infirmary (1833), now the Royal Bucks Hospital (see card 59). Robert Ceely F.R.C.S. continued in occupation until 1882. It was occupied by Dr Hilliard, also surgeon to the Infirmary. From 1902 to 1921 Dr John Baker practised from this house. Through the gateway adjoining can be seen a fine double coach house in original condition. One of the early motor cars in the town was to occupy one of the coach houses, and Mr Moxon the chauffeur was often to be seen polishing it in the courtyard. The remaining Georgian building is the County Museum, built in 1719 as a school, taken over as the museum in 1907 and extended into Ceely House in the late 1940's.

3. Here we see the continuation of the south west side from card 1, giving a more detailed view of first the Chantry, a 16th century building refronted 1840 – an impressive façade well worth careful inspection. In the 1860's this was the home of Robert Gibbs, author of the History of Aylesbury and many other books of local occurrences and history. He was editor of the Bucks Advertiser, a paper which still continues as strong an interest in Old Aylesbury. Our medical association of the street continues with Dr A.W. Coventon, who took over Dr Baker's practice in 1921 but changed its location to the Chantry. He was succeeded by Dr P. Gimson who continued here until 1975, and there finishes the street's medical association after nearly two centuries of unbroken service to the town. Number 10, the Georgian fronted building, was the home of Mr G.T. Hunt of Hunt Barnard's, one of the printers in the town whose works were in Buckingham Street from 1898 to 1927, then moving to a new factory in Stoke Road. Number 12, the 17th century bay-fronted cottage was the author's boyhood home. Next door, of the same period, was Bailey's dairy business – the only commercial premises in the street.

4. The Church War Memorial, erected in the churchyard by the main entrance from Church Street as you turn into Parson's Fee (which connects with Castle Street). All this area surrounding the church is part of the earliest town, extending to the Market Square, Kingsbury and adjacent streets. This card shows the unveiling ceremony.

PARSON'S FEE. AYLESBURY

1854

5. Parson's Fee. The houses in the foreground are the continuation of the Alms Houses in Church Street, and are part of a charity to provide homes for the poor and needy of the town. It was founded by Thomas Hickman who lived at number 1 Church Street in the 17th century. The 17th century cottages with over-hanging upper storeys were, in the early days of Queen Victoria's reign, a dame school conducted by Miss Turner. The title page of one of the Quarterly Reports is shown in number 6. The gateway at the turn of the cobbled street is the entrance to Prebendal House which in the mid-18th century was occupied by John Wilkes, editor of the radical North Briton, Member of Parliament for Aylesbury and a champion of liberty.

ESTABLISHMENT

FOR

YOUNG LADIES,

PARSONAGE FEE,

AYLESBURY,

BUCKS.

Miss Sarah Dickins

QUARTERLY REPORT

OF

Conduct, &c. &c.

From May 20th 1847

To

MARSHALL, PRINTER, AYLESBURY.

6. The Dame School, Parson's Fee. The title page shown is from a quarterly report which records the daily marks of a pupil under 21 headings — surely a most efficient record of progress and attainment. The following are extracts from the preface: *a Record is daily made of her application to the various subjects of study in which she is engaged. The figures opposite each branch of learning, there specified, are employed to denote different degrees of merit or demerit: 3, signifying a remarkably good Exercise, Copy, Recitation, etc.; 2, what is inferior, though not faulty; 1, that which calls for censure; while X denotes extreme negligence. ... Any violation of truth, propriety of language, etc is marked by the figures 1, 2, and 3, each expressing the degree of demerit... It is presumed that this Plan will meet the approbation of Parents...*

AYLESBURY, St MARY'S (PARISH CHURCH)

7. St Mary's Church dating from the early 13th century is cruciform, that is with chancel, nave and transepts; additions have modified the original lay-out but it still predominates. The Early English embattled tower with a corner turret is particularly massive and houses a belfry with eight bells. The earliest is dated 1612, the others 1773; all bear inscriptions. The lead clock tower and spire were added in the 17th century. Standing 120 feet high on the highest point of the town it is seen at considerable distance when approaching Aylesbury. The Lady Chapel has a Saxon vault below, marking the position of a church here long before the 13th century.

S 5002.　　　　　　　　　　ST. MARY'S CHURCH, INTERIOR, AYLESBURY.

8. The interior of St Mary's, looking towards the high altar with 3 stained glass lancet windows above. There are 9 windows in the chancel depicting scenes from the life of our Saviour. The carved figures of St Peter and St Paul are from Ober Ammergau. Note the fine Early English arches of the nave. The lighting shown is gas — originally bare fish-tail jets, later enclosed in globes — before the installation of electric lighting. There are aisles left and right. At the western end of the nave is a glorious stained glass window of 6 large lights depicting Noah, Abraham, Moses and David, with the 4 major prophets, 12 minor prophets and 6 scenes from the Old Testament.

9. Here we see the finely carved Norman font which is also evidence of an earlier church on this site. Originally in the south aisle, it was moved to the nave in recent extensive alterations. In the north transept is an impressive 16th century alabaster monument to Lady Lee; in the inscription is a request: *Good fre'd sticke not to strew with crims'o flowers. This marble stone wherein her cindres rest.* To this day the visitor will find fresh red flowers on the tomb. The worn marble figure of a knight in the recess was found in the grounds of the old Grey Friars monastery and is believed to be of Sir Robert Lee.

The Font in St. Mary's Church, Aylesbury.

Ladychapel Parish Church, Aylesbury.

10. The Lady Chapel at St Mary's was added in the 14th century. This was used as the old Latin school until 1720 when a new school was built in Church Street and the Latin school then moved into the Church Hall on the corner of Pebble Alley. This building again became a school during the Great War, taking overflow classes from St Mary's Church School in Oxford Road. The 18th century mahogany altar table is well shown, note the elaborate carving on the legs, and cherub heads in the centre. The chapel was restored in 1897. There was an extensive restoration of the church in 1848 when it was found to be in a dangerous state, only part then being used. It took twenty years to complete as even foundations had to be replaced.

11. St Mary's Church by night, illuminated for the peace celebrations of 19th July 1919 and seen from Pebble Alley which connects St Mary's Square with Kingsbury. Note the cobbled lane with its central gulley, the only other example surviving is in the alley from the old King's Head Inn to Temple Street. An old water pump still survives on the left, set very high on the wall for the filling of water carts which were used for spraying the streets in summertime to lay the dust. The Forester's Arms, another of Aylesbury's many pubs, is the oldest surviving building in the alley.

TEMPLE SQUARE AND CHURCH STREET AYLESBURY

12. Temple Square. The 18th century building marked St Mary's Church House was the headquarters of the Oxford and Bucks Light Infantry at the time of the First World War. The red brick house on the corner was the residence of Captain Nicholls the officer in command. The tiny railed garden has long since been removed. Behind these buildings with access to Church Street was the Drill Hall which provided overnight accommodation for many of the troops of Kitchener's Army passing through in the early days of the First World War. Photographs of the troops resting in the King's Head yard can be seen at the King's Head still. These were the days of hundreds of troops marching through the town in unbroken ranks which took hours passing through. Many rested overnight, had a quick bread and cheese breakfast and marched on again. These were the men who were to stand the first violent onslaughts of the war, the trench warfare and the great early losses of so many gallant men. This card is of the peaceful decade preceding those dark days. Church Street and the church are clearly shown.

13. Temple Square, with the premises of E.P. Gilkes, an old Aylesbury firm of builders, adjoining the Church House. The top of Castle Street is seen as far down as the 'Mount'. The inn sign is that of the Black Horse, one of Aylesbury's legion of lost pubs. The Georgian house to the left was Dr Taylor's during the first half of this century and the 18th century house adjoining, now known as Agriculture House, was the home of Mr Charles Hooper, a surgeon in the latter half of the 19th century; Dr T.G. Parrott became a partner in 1886. Also still in the square is the Queen's Head which dates from the 17th century. The large premises now occupied by Raffety Buckland, estate agents, was Thorp's, grocers and bacon factors, established in 1838. The bacon factory was on Rickford's Hill nearby. The first half of the present century saw many grocers, both large and small, in the town. Today there are only a few supermarkets, all the old family provision merchants, however long established, have disappeared – a change none could have foreseen.

CASTLE STREET, AYLESBURY

14. Castle Street. This card combines two views, the upper one depicting the top half of the street from Temple Square to the junction with Parson's Fee. The lower half is looking in the opposite direction. This was originally the only access to the town from Oxford, and for horse-drawn traffic must have been a severe climb. The levels of pavements and building line clearly shown in both views are interesting as they indicate considerable lowering of the original road level to make the ascent less arduous. The extension of Oxford Road through Duck End and Green End gave an easier approach. The terrain of this elevated area may indicate the site of an ancient castle which existed, and to which there are many clues, although not a single trace remains. Excavations in the 1970's revealed considerable evidence of fortifications and Tudor wells in the Bourbon Street and Temple Street area. All the public houses have now disappeared from Castle Street but most can still be remembered; from the first quarter of the century: The Black Horse, The Plume of Feathers, The White Lion, The Half Moon, and the Rising Sun at the junction with Oxford Road.

15. Temple Street, anciently known as Cordwainer's Street and Cobbler's Row, brings us now into the earliest trading area of the town, which extends to the Market Square, Kingsbury, and the adjacent streets and alleyways. This card depicts the street in the first decade of the present century. The fabric of most of the buildings is of early origin but being a street of shops has seen much alteration. Theobald's in the foreground was a china and glass store. The next shop, with the pendant gas lamp over the front was a stationers and newsagents, originally Shelton's and subsequently Richardson's. The adjacent building with bay windows on both floors is the Literary Institute. The last building on the right was Grinnell's leather shop with a tannery yard at the rear. Mr Grinnel put up the shutters and retired abruptly in 1922 and the shop was not entered again until the early years of the last war when it was found to be just as when trading had ceased twenty years before.

Temple Street, Aylesbury.

Market Street, Aylesbury

16. Turning left from Temple Street towards the Market Square we enter the very short and narrow Market Street. Even today it is still only wide enough for one vehicle at a time. On the right is the old shop front of G.M. Adams, the oldest established tobacconists in the town. It has since been completely rebuilt but still trades here, and in Kingsbury in even older premises. Wood's the florists – long since gone, and Smith's the butchers with Franklin's, drapers, on the corner, completes this side. On the other side was McIlroy's, then Duke's old established china and glass store extending down the Dark Lantern alley. Next was Watt's shoe shop and finally, on the corner with Silver Lane, Lee's the grocers, all replaced now with modern shops and offices.

Aylesbury. Market Square.

17. Market Square, looking down the square to the County Hall (built between 1720 and 1740) – a leisurely view of the early 1900's. From time immemorial the square has been the centre of life and activity, public occasions, and trading. A familiar figure in the square for many years was Jimmy Goodwin, a cripple who sold matches from a tricycle made for him by Kingham, a local cycle dealer. Another familiar character was Ted Cook, with his crutch and twisted leg, who sold papers in the square. 'Pigeon' Green and 'Peewit' were two other local odd-job men always in evidence. Freddie Fisher plied a fly-cab between the station and the hotels which surrounded the square, and was usually to be seen with one or two small boys riding free on the projecting rear axle, a safe perch at the gentle speed at which he drove. 'Whip behind, Freddie' was the call to warn him of his concealed passengers. The whip was long enough to dislodge them without harm. The iron railings which are evident in all scenes of the square for the past hundred years enclosed the open trading area and served to tether horses and cattle.

20456 Aylesbury. Market Square.

6. 8. 06.

18. This shows another view of the Market Square but in the opposite direction. The clock tower was erected in 1876. A horse sale is being conducted nearby, and there was ample convenient space for parking the horse-drawn vehicles at the centre of activities. The two fine recumbent iron lions on stone bases in the foreground were presented to the town by Baron Ferdinand de Rothschild of Waddesdon in 1888. On the right is Kingham's, a large grocery store, later to become Boots the Cash Chemists, next door was the International Stores, which moved to High Street and is no longer in the town. Next is Ancient & Armstrong, stationers and book sellers, later Armstrong's who published many of the early postcards of the town. Next is Poulton's, later Mark & Lee, high class fancy goods and stationers. The tall brick building is the National Westminster Bank on the corner leading to the Bull's Head and Hale Leys Square. Right at the top is the George Inn, seen in detail in card number 22.

19. Aylesbury Division, Bucks Voluntary Aid Church Parade 1912. The old shops shown are: Freeman, Hardy & Willis, boots and shoes; Arthur Watts shoe shop destroyed by fire in 1934; then the Maypole and the Home & Colonial Stores, both selling dairy products and no longer represented in the town; Foster Brothers, men's clothing, is still trading. The tall building at top left is McIlroy's, drapers, with another big store just across at the top of the square next to Field's the jewellers and clock-makers. Robert Scott on the corner of Market Street, tobacconists and cigar merchants, was originally Margesson Adams and reverted to R. Adams after the last war. Between Scott's and Thomas Field's is the cobbled entrance to the King's Head.

King's Head Gateway & Window   Aylesbury

20. The King's Head, a remarkably well-preserved Tudor inn built about 1450 and still largely in its original state. It retains its spacious courtyard, which was in earlier days probably surrounded with additional accommodation and galleries. It is now the last survivor of our ancient inns. The window, with its massive timbers and much original glass, must originally have looked out on to the Market Square, as all the buildings which hide it now, are of much later construction. For a time, while Adams' tobacconists was being rebuilt in 1962, it had again an unobstructed view of life in the square. One section of the upper lights which still contains the original stained glass, has the arms of Margaret of Anjou, wife of Henry VI, which confirms the period of the building. The Royal arms indicate that it may have been built as a Guild house. There was a Guild of Aylesbury established in 1425 which probably was its original owner.

Ye Olde King's Head Hotel, Aylesbury.　15th Century Room.　J. J. Widdowson, Proprietor.

21. The Great Hall at the King's Head. This is now the public bar and is a lofty room with the ceiling divided by heavy timbers meeting in a central boss and supported by massive beams. Part of the wall has been exposed to show the wattle and daub construction. In the winter a big log fire burns in the open fireplace. Every visitor to the town should take the opportunity to drink and talk in this ancient atmosphere where men have met and enjoyed their surroundings for centuries. Take the chance at the same time to sit in Cromwell's chair. 'The Glue Pot' is a small room to the side of the bar with seating for 6 to 8 people, ideal for quiet secluded conversation. Aylesbury was a parliamentarian town during the Civil War, and the King's Head would have seen many troops of the period, as much of the fighting occurred in the immediate vicinity; the Battle of Aylesbury was on the outskirts of the town in 1642 when Prince Rupert was routed by Sir William Balfore and John Hampden, and harassed in the rear by local townsmen. A full account of the battle is given in Gibbs' History of Aylesbury.

22. The George Hotel. On the north side is another of the remarkable number of very large inns which have, as far as records go back, always surrounded our Market Square. Nothing remains of the original 'George' which was 16th century and occupied the greater part of the upper square. It is recorded that a large election mob attacked and extensively damaged the building in 1784. It was rebuilt in the early 1800's and became a noted coaching inn. It was also greatly concerned throughout its history with politics and elections. Benjamin Disraeli, later Lord Beaconsfield, Queen Victoria's Prime Minister had many associations with it, and his statue was erected nearby. It was taken over eventually by the local Territorial Association, housing their guns and vehicles in the large yard at the rear which ran back to George Street. George Street was named after the old inn which was pulled down in the mid-thirties and the site rebuilt with modern shops. The only part to survive was the building to the left — T.R. Seaton, wine merchant — originally the public bar to the George, later the George Bodega, then just the Bodega (both run as bars), and now Seaton's again — but a wine bar.

The Square, Aylesbury

23. Looking across from the George, the building with 'Bradford' over and the low building in front was J.H. Bradford's, the town's largest ironmongers, and before then 'Sarsons'. These have now been replaced by shops and offices. This was the site of the old Black Swan, a half-timbered Tudor inn extending to 'back street' and well into Kingsbury. It survived, looking the ancient building it was, until 1883. The existence of so many large inns indicates a very busy, flourishing town with much through traffic and visitors throughout the centuries. The Round House 'King & Sainsbury's' gents and boys outfitters must have been one of the smallest shops in the town. To the left is Cambridge Street, formerly Bakers Lane on a map of 1809. To the right is High Street, not constructed until 1826 and then called New Road. This area was previously the Hale Leys meadows. The approach to Aylesbury from London before 1826 was via Walton.

24. The lamp post on the left was the position of the point-dury policeman controlling traffic until 1934 when traffic lights were introduced. The next hotel in the square was the Crown, again of 16th century origin and like all old inns quite extensive with its gardens, bowling green, stabling and yards. The card shows the rebuilt hotel as it still appeared in the 1920's, it was finally demolished in 1937 and was replaced by more shops. In the old days, before the New Road (High Street) was made, its frontage would have been across much of the upper square, the line of building then extending to the Bull's Head. The shops on the upper east side are all encroachments into the old square.

25. Market Square, upper east side. Here we see the shops referred to in number 24, the Vale Temperance Hotel, Spraggs the tailors (now in the High Street) afterwards S.G. Waters, next Wright's the chemists, succeeded by T.M. Ashford, Briggs boot and shoe store bringing us to the entrance to Hale Leys and the Bull's Head. The Aylesbury Fire Brigade parade of 1912 dates the period of the businesses shown.

AYLESBURY, MARKET SQUARE

59519

26. Sheep Market. Continuing from card number 25 we look across directly into Hale Leys Passage and the Bull's Head, yet another inn with 15th century origins. The timber front was an embellishment of the 1920's by Gargini, a well remembered landlord. The façade other than the 'timbering' is of the 18th century. It is possible that in the 17th century the inn was known as the Saracen's Head. The sheep and cattle markets held in the square gave way to market traders and their stalls in 1927. Fairs were still held there until 1938.

Aylesbury Town Hall & Lord Chesham's Statue.

27. The Town Hall and County Hall. This card shows the bottom of the Market Square (south), on the left are the arches of the Corn Exchange, on the right the County Hall. The arches and the Corn Exchange were built on the site of the old White Hart Inn, another 15th to 16th century inn on the Market Square. There was a central gateway to the courtyard and large well-kept gardens and pleasure grounds, stabling to the rear and a further building attributed to the Earl of Rochester in the reign of Charles II. Again there is history of the Civil War period concerning the escape of Royalists from the inn. For the love story of Grace Gilvey, the landlord's daughter, and her suitors, consult Gibbs' History where a long account is given in verse. The inn was rebuilt in 1814 and became one of the finest and most renowned hostelries outside London. It had only fifty years of success in the hands of J.K. Fowler, when, at great loss to the town, it was bought by the Aylesbury Market Company and demolished to build the Corn Exchange and Market in 1865. It was acquired by the Urban District Council in 1901 and became the Town Hall and Offices.

MARKET SQUARE, AYLESBURY.

28. It was a common practice in the early days of postcards, especially local views with a snow scene, to overprint with greetings and sell them as Christmas cards. Here we have a typical example showing the County Hall. This 18th century building is attributed to Sir John Vanbrugh, and contains the County Courts and Offices of the Clerk of the Peace. The iron-railed area of pavement in front was known as Debtor's Fee and prisoners were allowed to take exercise there. Public hangings took place from a drop erected on the balcony (1809) of the central first floor window until 1845. The balcony has long since gone. The south side is completed by the Bell which extends into Walton Street.

29. Passing under the Town Hall arches we approach the Cattle Market. The sale of livestock was discontinued in the Market Square in 1927 and the market stalls which had been confined to the lower part of the square expanded to occupy the whole available area. This is an early view of the cattle market before the erection of permanent pens, auctioneers offices, weighing machine etc. Access was also from Exchange Street which obviated cattle and sheep being driven in through the square. No longer did the Fire Brigade have to turn out to wash down the square after the sales. Loader's, the corn and agricultural merchants seen in our picture, disappeared to make way for the Civic Centre. The farmers and merchants were able to conduct all their business in a very compact area, and much business was conducted in adjacent public inns and hotels — mainly The Grapes, The Green Man, and The Bear in Walton Street — which on Wednesdays and Saturdays were solely farmers' pubs. The Bear, which had a smithy at the rear, has now gone.

Market Square, Aylesbury

30. This card shows the lower south west corner of the Market Square. Behind, and parallel with the buildings shown, ran Silver Street. All this area, together with Friarage Road, Silver Lane, Great Western Street, and the south side of Bourbon Street was entirely demolished in the 1960's to make way for the modern Friarage Square shopping centre. Goodridges dining rooms are clearly shown, then the Cross Keys and the Coach and Horses, both at least 18th century. Then came T.M. Ashford's who had moved from the far side of the square. Next was Troup's, seed merchants, and then the Old Beams which was the site of the White Horse Inn that in the 18th century faced on to the square. This gives us the original line of building again, continuing up to the Dark Lantern, a 16th century inn now hidden in the alleyways created by the encroachment of the shops, Jones & Cocks, Freeman, Hardy & Willis and those shown on the right in card number 35 to the top of the square.

31. The Market Square, 1870. From 1866 to 1876 the square presented a barren and empty picture for the first time in its history. Gone was the last market house and all the buildings which had occupied the centre. The clock tower, the statues and memorials had not yet been erected. The large drapery store in the right foreground, which preceded McIlroy's, was then Polden & Gurney, hence the carriage delivering ladies to the door.

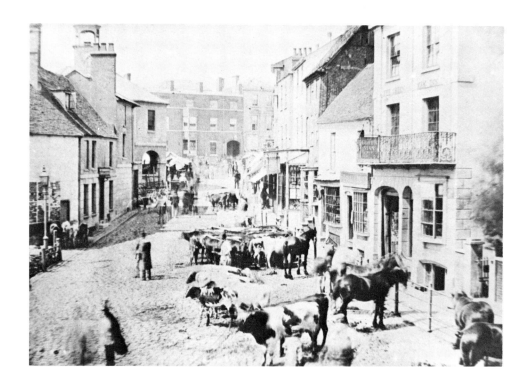

32. The Market House. This photograph, earlier than the postcards on which this record is based, is included to show the built-up state of the old square. The Green Man is well in evidence with an early Bucks Herald office next door. The pub sign is of the old Oxford Arms. The livestock market was obviously conducted anywhere there was space available around the many buildings that occupied most of the central area. The arched building at the top was the Market House, built in 1806 to replace the old market house which had stood on the site since 1530. It only endured until 1866 when the whole central area was cleared as can be seen in card number 31 of 1870.

33. This is the only photograph I have seen which shows the 1806-1866 market house with stalls around it. Aylesbury had one of the earliest public clocks, on an arm projecting from the 16th century market house, which was greatly missed when the building was demolished as 50 years elapsed before the addition of the one shown on the turret. This in turn disappeared with the building in 1866. This has been given by Mr Acton Tindal when he became Lord of the Manor. It was preserved and other sites sought for it. Eventually it was installed in the new clock tower, 1876, by public subscription, with faces on all four sides.

Market Square Aylesbury

MARKET DAY, AYLESBURY.

34. A Victorian scene showing the upper corner of the market, crowded and busy as always. On market days the carriers' carts came into town from all the surrounding villages, bringing people to do their weekly shopping. Each carrier had his particular inn where the cart would be left for the day, the villagers making repeated journeys to take their purchases back to the carts, and all aware of the time they must be there for the return journey.

35. An Edwardian market scene showing Wilson's grocery store on the left, which stood where the Midland Bank and Disraeli's statue now stand. It moved later into Kingsbury and, like most private grocery stores in the town, eventually disappeared. Note the ladies' large hats and costumes of the period, the men's knee breeches, and the popular straw boaters and stiff collars. The gas lamp shown reminds us that it was 23rd September 1834 when the streets were first illuminated; it was a gala day in the town with public cooking by gas and a celebration dinner at night at the White Hart.

36. A final, more modern, scene before the market was abolished and trading forbidden in the square. It was transferred to the new Friar's Square shopping centre, the building of which had destroyed so much of the old town. It was a sad loss after being for centuries the centre of town life and trading. The old market was a fascinating place, selling everything from sweets, fruit, clothing, plants, tools and every daily need. The cheapjacks, mock auctioneers, and 'here today — gone tomorrow' catch-penny traders providing much entertainment as well as cause for regret. A crowd formed around open stands to watch teeth extracted with bare fingers, or corns removed. Marvellous remedies were offered for the instant relief of all ailments.

37. The unveiling of the Lord Chesham Memorial on 14th July 1910 and obviously a fine summer day for the occasion. Major General Sir Charles Compton, later Lord Chesham, founded the Bucks Company of the Imperial Yeomanry, and served with distinction during the Boer War under Field Marshal Lord Roberts V.C.

38. A close-up of the ceremony to give more detail of the statue; the sculptor was John Tweed. All the statues in the Market Square are fine examples of work by well-known sculptors. Lord Roberts is seen to the left in the plumed head-dress of a Field Marshal, beside him is Lord Rothschild, Lord Lieutenant of the County.

39. The Royal Bucks Hussars on parade for the unveiling. Lord Roberts is seen inspecting and talking to veterans of the South African War. Mr Millburn, with plate camera is waiting to photograph the occasion. Most of the early local postcards are the work of Mr Millburn, and earlier of S.G. Payne & Son. The buildings in the background are the International Stores which took the site of Longleys shop; Boots the Chemists and The Green Man.

40. The ceremony of laying the foundation stone of the John Hampden memorial was part of the coronation festivities of 22nd June 1911. Current coins of the realm, the coronation programme, local papers and other documents were deposited beneath the stone. The local children, marshalled in school groups sang 'Land of Hope and Glory' and the National Anthem, led by Aylesbury Printing Works Band. They were presented with souvenir medallions given by Field's the jewellers, and afterwards entertained to a big tea in the Town Hall. The committee and their ladies took tea at Walton Grange at a charge of 9 pence per head.

41. The unveiling of the statue of John Hampden, 27th June 1912, a year later than the laying of the foundation stone. The statue was presented by Mr James Griffin of Long Marston to perpetuate the memory of a great patriot, and at the same time to celebrate the Coronation of George V and Queen Mary. There are two plaques of scenes – the Battle of Chalgrove Field, and the burial of Hampden – and two of inscription. The final words of the plaque headed John Hampden are a concise assessment:

Against my King I do not fight
But for my King and Kingdom's right

Hampden Statue, Aylesbury.

42. An excellent view of the John Hampden statue circa 1912. The boys are in the typical dress of the period, and the statue has already become a gathering point for those with time to spare. John Hampden is pointing to his birthplace. It was his refusal to pay the unjust tax — Ship Money — levied by Charles I which contributed to the Civil War. He raised the local force of 'Greencoats' for Parliament, and fought through all the early stages of the war until he was wounded at the Battle of Chalgrove Field on 18th June 1643. He died of his wounds six days later at the Greyhound Inn in Thame, the town where he had received his early education at the Lord Williams Grammar School. He was buried at Great Hampden Church. Aylesbury was a garrison town for the Parliamentary forces; the powder magazine was in St Mary's Church which suffered much damage from Cromwell's forces, as did many churches at that time.

43. Queen Victoria's Jubilee celebrations in the Market Square 1897. There were only the Rothschild lions and a horse trough at the bottom of the square then. The clock tower 1876 was the first building to occupy the square after the clearance of the Market Hall and buildings seen in number 32. Kingham & Sons, provision merchants, and Longleys, drapers, are more clearly shown here than in any other cards of the period. The change to International and Boots are seen in card number 39. Modern shops have replaced these but the upper storeys remain unaltered. Rowe & Company became Jones & Cocks, still as ironmongers. Were summers better in the old days? All our Aylesbury celebrations seem to have been particularly fortunate in their weather.

44. 'Lest We Forget.' The Great War Memorial extends the whole width of the upper market place to the Hampden statue. Unveiled in 1921 to the glorious memory of the local men who fell in the First World War. 264 names are recorded on bronze plaques across the width. The memorial was provided by local subscription and was based on the design of those erected in British Cemeteries in France. A further 106 names were added in 1951, of those who fell in the Second World War.

45. Silver Street. On the right many of the buildings are the backs of premises in the Market Square (see card number 30), for example The Cross Keys. All these buildings, with those on the left comprising the old Silver Street were swept away in the development of the sixties. On the left was the Greyhound Inn, Marshall's the jewellers, Hewitt's the butchers, Wood's, opticians, Pither's six and a half penny bazaar, and Aylesbury's first Co-op shop. At the top is Jones & Cocks hardware warehouse, later to be converted to retail premises when they moved out of the square. Silver Lane also disappeared in the alterations; this ran parallel with Bourbon Street and joined Friarage Hill behind the swimming baths which were built on the site of the old Dell's brewery. The lane was in a very poor state with only one or two cottages inhabited and other buildings used for storage. All the south side of Bourbon Street was demolished at the same time, including M.T. Cocks, high class grocers, the old Bucks Advertiser & Aylesbury News offices, Flitney's the bakers, the St John ambulance station, and the fire brigade station.

Kingsbury Square.
Aylesbury

46. Kingsbury, adjoining the Market Square, keeps us in the ancient town centre, and then, Royal Borough. The Manor House probably extended across the whole north face. It was held by William the Conqueror and continued in Royal possession until King John who granted it to Geoffrey Fitz Piers. It passed by marriage to Sir Thomas Bullen, father of Lady Ann Bullen or Boleyn – the 'Fair Maid of Aylesbury' – who became the second wife of Henry VIII. No traces remain of the Manor House, only its documentation through the ages. The buildings occupying its site are of various periods from 17th century to modern, as can be seen in the card which is pre-1920. Fleet's Basket Works and shop is on the extreme left. The next shop was Fisher's the butchers, and then Samuel's Printing Works with the ornate gable. The big garage and service depot must have been well ahead of its time as the lettering across the roof announces 'Aeroplanes Repaired'. The small shop next door was Rutland's the bakers. All these businesses have long since gone.

47. Our next card completes the scene to the left, showing the 17th century Rockwood Inn. In the left foreground is the Red Lion, a 16th century inn of which part of the usual central gateway to the courtyard can be seen. Similar gates at the rear opened into George Street which in old records is Hogg Lane. It is still an inn and popular dining place, though much altered; the gates are gone and the courtyard built over. Anne Rogers who sold beer there in 1569 would hardly recognise it. The shop on the corner was Mackrill's, electricians, next was Killer's monumental masons yard and workshops, and then the Victoria Working Mens' Club 1887. Deliveries are being made by horse and cart, various tradesmen's handcarts and an errand boy complete with apron and basket can be seen. For many years in the mid-19th century the cattle market was held in Kingsbury.

48. This card of 1920 shows a tank being driven up the High Street en route for Kingsbury where a concrete base had been prepared for it to go on display. Many people did not want any reminder of the Great War, but it looked better than the galvanised-iron temporary public convenience which had stood there during the war. St Mary's Church School released its pupils (a wartime generation) early that afternoon so that they might see the tank arriving.

49. Here we see the tank officially installed and the crowds that had gathered for the ceremony. The tank remained until 1929 when it was cut up on the spot with acetylene torches. Enough petrol had survived in one of the tanks to blow-up when the torch was turned on it; parts were picked up in the gardens behind the houses in the picture. The tank had been a centre of attraction for small boys who climbed all over it, and eventually gained access to the interior as well. Mr Millburn, auctioneer, who had a saleroom in Cambridge Street, used to conduct sales of household goods in the open air in Kingsbury. The goods would be laid out in rows and he moved along the lots, using a wooden chair to stand on so that he could see the bids being made. The little shop in the extreme left corner was Higgins' sweet shop, catering for a juvenile trade only. It was later incorporated into the Rockwood.

KINGSBURY, AYLESBURY

50. We now move to the east side of Kingsbury looking towards the Market Square. The first shop on the left was the Bonnet Box, ladies and babies wear, now Adams Travel Agency; many of the early emigrants to Canada booked here. Adams the tobacconist is still there and is the oldest established in the town. Next was Clark's newsagents where we bought our comics. It became part of Ivatts, the shoe shop next door. Robert Ivatts opened in 1723 in the reign of George II, and it continued as a family business until the seventh generation. In 1949 an old-established Norwich firm of shoe retailers took over after 226 years of uninterrupted trading by Ivatts. The name remained over the shop, celebrating two and a half centuries of trading in 1973. The premises have only just been vacated. The white-fronted shop was Ware's the butchers. Next we see the sign of the Eagle, another 17th century inn, which survived until 1975.

51. Continuing the east side of Kingsbury we show F.B. Rawlings, stationers and booksellers, Narbeth's, drapers, and Gulliver's Wine Stores after the disastrous fire of 24th May 1913. Gulliver's was restored and continued trading for many years. Narbeth's moved into the High Street where they had two shops. All the premises on this side of the square extended into Back Street which always looked like 'back' premises, no attempt being made to keep up appearances. Rubbish was dumped there and allowed to accumulate in the days before town refuse was collected.

52. This card shows the continuation of shops viewed from the opposite end. From the Market Square was Bradford's iron-mongers, now gone. Next was Jowett's, also ironmongers, taken over by Mr Philby when Mr Jowett retired and continued by him under the old name until 1984. Wheeler's, bakers and pastrycooks, adjoined, next was Pearks', which like the Home & Colonial Stores and the Maypole sold mainly butter, cheese, eggs and tea. None were grocers dealing in all foodstuffs. The high fascia beyond the sun-blinds was Francis' hardware shop, the rear of the premises into Back Street was run as a penny bazaar. On the left is the sign of the Angel, another ancient inn; the site remained empty for many years after its demolition early this century but the sign survived and was transferred to the Victoria and Albert Museum in London. Mr Honour, the carrier for Bierton and Hulcott 'put up' at the Angel on Wednesdays and Saturdays and continued using the site long after the inn was dismantled.

53. A parade through Kingsbury circa 1908 featured all the local fire brigades: the Aylesbury Volunteer, Aylesbury Printing Works, and Waddesdon and Halton, both Rothschild estate brigades. The array of banners are difficult to identify, but the Ancient Order of Foresters and Loyal Vale of Aylesbury Lodge can be seen. Two types of bracket gas lamps are shown, these were the private lamps used on the more important shops of the period. Street lamps were sparsely distributed. The small butchers over to the right later became Wheeler's corn and seed stores, with a double window front. Beyond, the derelict remains of the Angel can be seen, and on the corner the Bank Building, now Lloyds.

54. Looking down Back Street which runs parallel with Kingsbury. It is the continuation of Buckingham Street, also known as Back Buckingham Street. It was possible then for tradesmen to discuss business in the middle of the street, while poultry foraged for scraps. They were released into the street from the cellar flap seen on the right. The gentleman with the top hat is Mr Jenns from the furniture shop further down Buckingham Street. The state of the roads and cobbled pavements – even in the squares – left much to be desired, especially in winter. Note the decrepit state of the buildings on the right. The first building on the left is part of Sale Brothers, grocers. The Two Brewers was the pub used by the carriers' carts from Oving. Mr Clark (carrier) came to Aylesbury on Wednesdays and Saturdays, Mr Elmer came daily. The shop with the sun-blind was H. Sale's, cabinet maker and picture framer, and brother of the grocers. The house with the four trees in front was Turner's the dentist. All of these buildings are now demolished.

55. This is the lower half of Back Street in the winter of 1908. J. Bryant's shoe shop was between The Harrow and The Barley Corn in Cambridge Street; it was pulled down years ago and the site remained empty until the Aylesbury Brewery Company joined the two pubs by building a mutual entrance across the gap. It was particularly well done and looks as if it has always been there. All the work done to their premises, whether re-building or extending, is always in excellent taste and perfect keeping with its locality. The combination of the old Crown Inn and Bull's Head into the new Bull and Crown is another fine example.

56. Back Street again, after the Kingsbury fire of 1913. This shows the basic construction of the buildings on this side of the street. Referring back to card 54, note the survival of 18th century cottages on the right, forming a marked contrast with the buildings opposite. It is still largely undeveloped.

Buckingham Street, Aylesbury

57. Buckingham Street from its junction with Kingsbury. To the left was the 'Little Wonder', a secondhand furniture shop kept by Mr Mealing, this, with adjoining houses, is now all new shops. R.W. Locke, brick manufacturer's office was here; the brick yards were at Hartwell, about two miles out, on the Oxford Road. Locke's bricks are to be seen in many Aylesbury buildings, with impressed dates and initials back to the early 1800's. The Buckingham Arms, another inn with ample courtyard accommodation, is seen on the right. Carriers' carts to Grandborough, Grendon, North Marston, Quainton and Whitchurch operated from here, a busy yard.

BUCKINGHAM STREET AYLESBURY

58. Continuing the line of shops was Plater's gents outfitters, Miss Peskett's, ladies outfitters, and Mead Brothers, seen outside their grocery shop; none of the many grocers we have seen, however long established, were to survive the advent of the modern supermarkets. Next, the shop with the balcony above, was Jenns & Sons, one of the largest furnishers in town, they manufactured their own bedding, buying the feathers from local farmers. The Wesleyan Methodist Church was built in 1893-94. Old cul-de-sacs off the Buckingham Road were Fisher's Yard and Cooper's Yard.

ROYAL BUCKS HOSPITAL, AYLESBURY.

59. The Royal Bucks Hospital, originally the Bucks Infirmary, was adapted first from a large house at the top of the hill where the roads from Bicester and Buckingham meet. Two wings were added in 1833. It was rebuilt largely under the supervision of Sir Henry Verney of Claydon, with much advice and guidance from Florence Nightingale (the 'Lady with the Lamp') of Crimean War fame. The foundation stone was laid in 1861 and the new hospital opened in 1862. The generosity, keen interest and loyal service of Dr Lee at Hartwell and Sir Harry are remembered in the naming of two of the wards. The early surgeons all gave their consulting services free, the first being the Ceely brothers previously referred to in Church Street (card number 2). Robert Ceely was affectionately remembered by rich and poor alike. A bust of Florence Nightingale is in the entrance hall.

VIEW OF AYLESBURY FROM MILL TAIL.

60. Entering Aylesbury from the Oxford Road we cross the bridge at Mill Tail and are immediately introduced to the famous Aylesbury duck. This remarkable table bird, which carries the town's name, was bred in great profusion. The meadow shown was known as 'Tommy Locke's' and from the stream and field, at the beginning of the century, teatime would see whole flocks on the Oxford Road 'going home'. At the foot of Whitehill one contingent would turn off to the breeders there, the main flock continuing right until the next batch turned off up Castle Street, the main batch finally turning down Mount Street to 'Duckie Weston's' – the biggest breeder of all. Not surprisingly, this part of the town was known as Duck End.

White Hill, Aylesbury.

61. The foot of Whitehill, at the same period as our last card, showing cobbled gulleys and pathways, and of course — ducks. There were only a few rural cottages here; carts could be left by the roadside overnight. Mr Stanley, general dealer, can be seen packing up for the day. The rest of the hill, on both sides, was flanked with high walls enclosing, on the left, the Roscoe estate, and on the right, the Prebendal. This area was originally known as Common Dunghill; common indicates open or common land on the outskirts of the town; Dunghill is probably a corruption of Dunge-hill from Dungeon Hill, a likely rear access to our lost castle, particularly as it runs parallel with Castle Street.

62. The foot of Whitehill where the Oxford Road turns right toward Castle Street. The building on the left with the fascia board was the now-forgotten Seven Stars public house. Behind the cottages on the right, extending along the Oxford Road, ran Ludd's Alley, a narrow lane of tiny cottages, none later than 1700 and named, it was believed, after Ludd's lodging house, but there was a Ludd's Fee in mediaeval times.

63. The continuation of Oxford Road showing the turn left into Castle Street. The gabled building (left foreground) is part of the Hen & Chickens public house, kept then by Thomas Locke who owned the meadow opposite running down to Mill Tail. It has since been pulled down and rebuilt as a larger modern public house still called the Hen & Chickens.

64. A photograph by S.G. Payne & Son of the cottages then adjoining the Hen & Chickens. Circa 1900, this photograph is included to show the remarkable quality attained with the plate cameras of the day. The name 'Locke' is seen on the old Hen & Chickens. Note the unusual barge boards. These cottages were in the gap seen in the previous card where the lady is leaning on the gate. Looking through the gate a large ammonite is seen below the window, these were from the nearby Hartwell quarries and are to be seen in the walls surrounding Hartwell Estate.

65. The Rising Sun, another 17th century pub, at the foot of Castle Street and facing along the Oxford Road. This was demolished with adjacent barns and the area incorporated with the old Mount to form raised gardens and grass areas with seats at the top – a pleasant place to rest in the sun. It overlooks the part previously referred to as Duck End, and looks down Mount Street, a cul-de-sac running down to the stream which bordered the big duck farm, and ran on, first to serve the mill at Mill Close, then on to the Mill Tail, under the road bridge, and then by the Pightle into the fields beyond.

AYLESBURY FROM THE MEADOWS.

66. This rural scene shows how abruptly the town finished at Oxford Road. To the right is St Mary's Church School, built 1845, but here we see only the Headmaster's house with the tall triple chimneys. In the early twenties the top of the field was divided into individual plots, and each pupil from the upper class had a garden to cultivate under the Headmaster's personal supervision. Not only was gardening taught, but the beginnings of trading also. The seeds were provided and paid for from the potatoes sold. All other produce, radishes, spring onions, beet, lettuces and peas were sold by the pupils from their own gardens, to their own profit. The school produce was eagerly sought by local residents and daily orders were collected on the way to school, and delivered on the way home. Mr H. Smiter A.C.P., the Headmaster, was an enthusiastic teacher; often the pupils were late going home as time was forgotten, and lessons terminated abruptly when the master was the first to realise they had over-run. He personally ran evening classes for pupils who had left school, and they were always well-attended. He is still remembered with respect and affection.

AYLESBURY. "DUCKS"

67. A final card on the ducks, circa 1910, and published by C. Armstrong, stationers of Market Square. The caption on the back reads: *Aylesbury Ducks. Aylesbury is the capital of Buckinghamshire, and is about 40 miles from London. It easily takes first place among the market towns of England; the supplies of agricultural and dairy produce to London being immense. Our view shows one of the duck farms for which Aylesbury is especially noted.*

68. The upper part of the High Street circa 1910, looking towards the Market Square with the George Hotel in the distance. Note the gas lamps, both bracket and standard, and the barber's pole on the left. The shops from the top were W.E. Adams, grocers, Allen's, greengrocers and fruiterers, Thrasher's, gents outfitters, Spragg's, and Jarvis', both ladies outfitters, and Hopcraft's wholesale and retail confectioners. This street did not exist before 1826 and was originally mainly private houses, the conversion to shops is still evident in many instances, more so on the west side lower down where single-storey shops were built over the front gardens.

Aylesbury. High Street.

20458

69. Continuing down the same side from our previous card, not shown is the National Westminster Bank, originally the Union of London and Smith's Bank. Next is Narbeth's drapery store running through to Cambridge Street. Mr Narbeth will long be remembered as an enthusiastic and outspoken member of our local council – a rebel who would not sink his principles. Next was F. Pass and the Aylesbury Carriage Works, later to become the first site of Woolworth's stores, one of the first big chain stores in Aylesbury. Even that was to disappear when they transferred to even larger premises in Walton Street. The line of shops from the left foreground (with the baskets out front), down to Longley's big store on the corner of Britannia Street are all gone. There was Hermon's, men's and boys' outfitters – a small shop with a big trade, Riching's dining rooms and Wood's opticians and chemists.

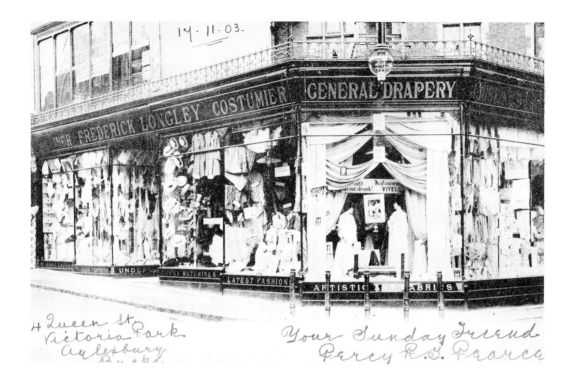

70. A close-up of F. Longley's, drapers, a remarkable shop and one of the largest in the town in its day, with accommodation for its assistants in houses opposite and in the cul-de-sac alongside. This was common practice with the larger Victorian shops, to provide staff with accommodation and their keep in their own dining rooms. Male and female staff were in separate premises of course! Shops then stayed open late into the evenings and the working day was really long. At its worst in London shops, assistants even slept under the counters.

71. Turning along Britannia Street, on the corner of Station Street was another of Aylesbury's lost pubs, the Ark. I have included this card to show the hey-day of the bill-sticker. The Ark was already closed and empty and presented a wonderful opportunity for the bill-poster with his ladders, brushes and cans of paste. They would plaster posters anywhere, particularly on derelict and empty properties. There were bill-posting companies who had huge wooden hoardings for the purpose around town; there was a big one for many years at the top of Tommy Locke's field in Oxford Road. They were often sited around railway stations.

High Street, Aylesbury.

72. Looking back up the High Street from the junction with Exchange Street, we see on the left the Chandos which has only recently disappeared to make way for still more offices. Next was Cook's newsagents and several small shops which changed hands fairly frequently. Then came the galvanised-iron Roman Catholic Church built in 1892 and replaced by the present church in 1937. The row of three-storey houses eventually all had single-storey shops extended across the front gardens. Ward & Cannon had an open-fronted builder's yard facing on to the High Street. Dr Dale's house stood back with a garden in front. Ward's wholesale tobacconist was another shop built across the garden, next was the first site of W.H. Smith's, newsagents, with the General Post Office, circa 1890, opposite Britannia Street.

Sunday 26-4-08

73. The snow storm of 26th April 1908 is featured on many Aylesbury cards. Here we see the lower High Street at the junction with Exchange Street. Three postmen in the uniform of the time are on their way back to the Post Office. To the left was the Aylesbury Gas Company showrooms and works. A fine standard gas lamp is seen on the left. A large gas holder stood in the yard and coke and tar was retailed there. Gas street lighting was introduced in 1834. The shop on the far corner of Exchange Street was Oliver's cycle store where they sold and hired cycles and also did replating and enamelling. The open area to the left extended right across to Park Street and was used for growing osiers for the Basket Works; it is now the Vale Park.

High Street, Aylesbury

74. This view up the High Street below Longley's clearly shows the conversion of private houses to shops. Some continued without alteration as dentists, namely Nurick's, Shuker's and Chilton's all in this area. S.G. Payne & Son, succeeded by Mr M.C. Millburn, at the corner shop opposite the General Post Office, were the early photographers in the town, producing many of the fine view cards that are now our best record of past times and places. All are now replaced by modern shops. The streets were safer places in those days for children as well as adults, with only horse-drawn traffic and cycles. It was then possible to play with marbles, tops and hoops in the streets. Shops displayed goods, not only on the pavements, but on the roadside as well. Ironmongers particularly would stand larger items of merchandise in the gutters.

75. The New Road (completed in 1826) which was to become the High Street, for the first time gave direct access to the town from Tring. Previously the only way in was off the Tring Road near Broughton pastures, cutting across to Wendover Road near the New Inn, and continuing up Walton Street to the bottom of the Market Square. The first buildings in New Road as we have seen were private houses, all to change to shops and become the main shopping thoroughfare, so much so that few realise it is of such recent origin compared with the rest of the old town. It was such a direct short-cut that it took most of the traffic from Walton Street. The muddy state of the road is shown in this card. In the left foreground is A.T. Adkins, established 1876, Aylesbury's largest cycle shop which still deals, in modernised premises, in cycles and motor cycles. The lower floors of the houses on the left are mainly converted to small shops facing the Vale Park.

HIGH STREET, AYLESBURY   NO 3

76. Approaching the canal bridge from our last card the left side is undeveloped and rural; on the right the houses begin to peter out and remain today much the same. The turning right is Albion Street, a cul-de-sac with cottages on both sides. Over the bridge begins the industrial development of the late 19th century.

The Canal, Aylesbury.

77. Pausing on the High Street bridge and looking south-west the arm of the canal which finishes at Walton Street can be seen. Opened in 1814, it connected Aylesbury with the Grand Union canal system which was transporting heavy goods at reasonable cost; it halved the cost of coal in the district. The town had previously relied on the Wendover branch opened in 1797, but this entailed the unloading of heavy or baulky goods and transport by road into Aylesbury, thus increasing the cost. Now goods could come into wharves in the town centre. Local produce could be transported to London or even to the North if time was not a prime factor. Coronation Villas on the left were built in 1902, hence the name. The cottages on the right, Willowbank Terrace, were originally planned to face Highbridge Walk but actually face the canal. They were built in 1903 and are the only dwellings on that side until we reach the basin with its wharves. The timberyards were located here on the arrival of the canal, and the Electricity Works boiler house stood alongside the basin handy for coal deliveries.

Canal and Milk Factory, Aylesbury

78. From the bridge looking in the opposite direction we see the Milk Factory on the right and Hills & Partridge Flour Mill on the left. This demonstrates the great advantage of canal transport where goods could be unloaded right at the factory wharf. We are looking up the arm to Marsworth, where it connected with the Grand Union canal, a distance of just over six miles. With 16 locks and 19 bridges, the construction was completed in 1814, having taken three years. The Park Street bridge was rebuilt about 1900, and just through the arch is the last lock on the arm.

79. Over the canal bridge there were no buildings until the erection of the Aylesbury Condensed Milk Company factory in 1870. This was the first factory producing the new condensed milk in the country. From 7 o'clock in the morning a continual stream of carts would begin arriving with milk from the farms. A rigid inspection would be made of every delivery. The factory was taken over by the Anglo-Swiss Company who already produced condensed milk in their Swiss factories. Later it became the Nestlé and Anglo-Swiss Condensed Milk Company. Our card is dated 1900; note the heavily wooded scene opposite at that time.

High Street, Aylesbury.

80. Eight years later than the previous card and note the change of scene, on the right the trees are all gone and we have a long row of villas extending almost to Walton Road and completing the development of the High Street. We now have a better view of the Milk Factory which covers the whole area bounded by the canal, High Street and Park Street as far as the bridge.

81. A photograph taken at the completion of the Milk Factory premises. Note the high quality brickwork of all, especially the boundary wall and the chimney. The High Street is on the left, and St Mary's Church spire can be seen in the distance. The rural area at this end of the High Street was not developed until 1908. Park Street, with its canal bridge, joins from the right. Hazell, Watson & Viney also opened their new factory in this area in 1878.

82. The unveiling of Hazell, Watson & Viney's War Memorial on 20th November 1920 in the garden on the corner of High Street and Walton Road, just across from their factory. Recent road alterations and the construction of a new roundabout destroyed the garden and the memorial tablets were incorporated in the walls of the new factory entrance on the corner of Park Street.

Printing Works and Tring Road, Aylesbury.

83. Hazell, Watson & Viney Printing Works, showing the machine room extension before the upper storeys were added. We are now at the start of Tring Road. The printing works first came to Aylesbury in 1867, taking over the old silk mill at California, and expanding into a new factory in Tring Road in 1878. The old factory was retained as the 'Ink Works'. The firm grew and prospered, every ten years seeing more additions and extensions, until, by the Great War, they were probably the largest employers of labour in the town.

84. 'Going to Work' at Hazell, Watson & Viney's in 1886. Note the undeveloped site opposite and in the previous card. Eventually, having completely occupied the area on the original site, building commenced opposite and continued to expand until now it houses all departments in a modern factory, and all the substantial Victorian factory and offices have only recently been demolished (1984) and the site disposed of.

85. Aylesbury Printing Works fire brigade outing 25th July 1906, ready to move off from the office entrance. Mr Roche the Fire Brigade Chief can be seen by the rear wheel having seen all safely aboard. The brigade equipment, like everything Hazell's did, moved with the times, and became an important back-up to the town's brigade. The firm's band appeared at all local occasions and was, by 1890, well-established and in uniform.

86. Aylesbury Printing Works Institute sports day, July 1911, with a demonstration by their fire brigade in progress. Caps, bowler hats and the ever-popular straw boaters are in evidence. Bank Holidays were instituted in 1871 and Hazell's sports were to become the town's biggest August Bank Holiday attraction.

87. A photograph of the top of Walton Street where it joins the Market Square by the Bell Hotel in 1902. The triumphal arch is to celebrate the Coronation of King Edward VII and Queen Alexandra. Mr Slade wears the uniform of Town Crier and is carrying the hand bell which would be rung preceding his announcements. On the left is Mr King who was sexton of St Mary's and a porter at Mr Millburn's saleroom in Cambridge Street. On the corner is Chapman's newsagents and tobacconists, better remembered later as Samuel's, then Feasey's. Through the arch is Fowler's Wine Stores, later the Victoria Wine Company. Next is Lucas' the pawnbrokers, a type of business which flourished in Victorian and Edwardian times and seldom seen now. It was pawnbrokers who helped the poor survive from week to week in the old days. Next was Cannon, Green & Company, builder's shop and yard, then Paragreen's, leather merchants. Walton Cottage can just be seen, an early 18th century house with fine bay windows on both floors. Beyond was The Old House, an impressive building of the 18th century. All this side of the street was swept away by the development of the early 1960's.

88. The same part of Walton Street as in the previous card, showing troops marching by in September 1913 on their way to camp. The weather must have been good that September as they had shed their tunics and rolled their sleeves up. The men were reported as the Bedford Regiment, but the badge does not look right. They are happy enough here, but in twelve months they were to be marching in earnest, as war was declared in August 1914. These were the men who were to take the brunt of the early offensives. We were reputed to be little prepared for this war, but the manoeuvres of 1913 were certainly on a large scale and attended by many of the 'top brass'.

89. The old Green & Company buildings were replaced with a smart new shop — Cannon, Green & Company — built in green glazed brick. This was also demolished in the 1960's. On the opposite side of Walton Street the Bell, the White Swan and the former Bucks Herald office were to survive, but all the other buildings down to the corner of Exchange Street, with the exception of Wilkins & Sons old offices, were demolished to make way for the new County Offices opened in 1929. These were built by Webster & Cannon who were responsible for most of the fine buildings erected in the town during this period. The old Police Headquarters on this corner and in Exchange Street is another typical example. The Clock Tower, the John Hampden Memorial and the War Memorial are also their work.

90. Moving on down Walton Street, beyond the junction with Exchange Street: on the corner was the old Cogger & Hawkins garage which later moved to new premises across Walton Street; these too have now gone to be replaced by Aylesbury's most modern building – the headquarters of Equitable Life Assurance – almost all glass, and known locally as 'the Blue Leanie'. The Ship, built 1815, marks the end of the canal and was built as soon as the canal was completed. This photograph shows the old Aylesbury Brewery Company Malt House, now replaced by a modern garage and office buildings. The Brewery Headquarters are on the same site but stand well back from the road. Here we see one of the contestants in the Harrow to Aylesbury Walking Race (thirty miles), 1st August 1903, passing the Brewery. The finish was at the top of Walton Street and the race was won by Mr Roche in 5 hours 26 minutes, all the other competitors took over 6 hours. Long distance walking races were very popular in the early part of the century and invariably started and finished at a public house.

Walton Street, Aylesbury

91. Walton Street from Holy Trinity Church. The house in the left foreground stood on the site now occupied by Holy Trinity Church Hall, built in 1927. The church was first suggested in 1839 and was built under financial difficulties and not consecrated until 1845. Money remained short and only a small stipend was available. The church income by 1848 was about £130 a year. The congregation was largely from the poor of the parish. The second minister appointed was the Reverend W. Pennefather who came, direct from Ireland, to find a parish of very poor people, mostly engaged in duck-rearing, straw-plaiting and lace-making. The canal than was a busy centre and many cottages were occupied by canal workers. The church soon concerned itself with providing a school for the poor children, who were receiving no education. The Reverend E. Holland, one of the trustees, bought two small houses near the church to provide a school. This was done long before a parsonage was provided. By 1849 the church was filled to capacity and had to be extended.

WALTON, SHOWING TRINITY CHURCH.

Leaving for Rickmansworth on Thursday

will write when I get there

92. Walton Street, the same area as the last card but viewed from the opposite direction. Quite large houses occupied the street on one side only, as can be seen in this, and in the previous, card. Again (as in Castle Street) we have a very elevated pavement due to reducing the road level to make the hill easier for horse traffic. Several of the houses still have coach-houses which are now several feet above road level. Walton, which had originally been a small hamlet now adjoined the town. Old alleyways and cul-de-sacs off Walton Street were Long Row, Gunners Row, Chapel Row, and Prospect Place opposite the Church Hall; all contained small cottages and constituted a very poor quarter.

WALTON POND,

Hope you are better, shall be pleased to

hear from you again
800.10. 92. 92.

93. Turning left at the end of Walton Street is Walton Road, an ancient highway to Bierton. The village aspect is still discernable, with the old Walton Pond in the picture still surviving. The ubiquitous Aylesbury duck is seen enjoying the quiet rural surroundings. One large 17th century farmhouse still stands along the road, completely unaltered. Walton Green and Walton Place have disappeared in modern road developments.

Walton Pond, Aylesbury.

94. One more view of Walton Pond is included as it shows the villas which replaced the old cottages seen in our last card, which in turn disappeared overnight when a land mine was dropped nearby during the Second World War. Also damaged by the bomb was Walton Grange, a fine 16th century farmhouse, but part of the walls and gateway still stand. The Aylesbury High School for Girls now occupies the bombed area.

9373 NEW SECONDARY SCHOOLS, AYLESBURY.

95. Further along Walton Road, on the right, is shown the Grammar School built in 1906. The old school from Church Street transferred to it, and the Church Street premises (built in 1719) became the museum. Like the council school in nearby Queen's Park, it was used to accommodate convalescent troops during the Great War. The Boys Grammar School has since been greatly extended over an area bounded by Hazell's, the Cemetery and Turnfurlong. This, together with the Girls High School now occupies all this side of the road up to the pond.

96. A postcard used for advertising. Many cards were issued by makers of well-known products such as Pear's Soap, Camp Coffee, Fry's Cocoa, Raleigh Cycles, Colman's Starch, Lipton's Tea and Quaker Oats to name but a few. Here we have an example of local advertising by H. Sale of Buckingham Street, picture frame maker, of the early twenties.

POST CARD

F. Longley's Drapery Series, High Street, Aylesbury.

This space may be used for Inland correspondence.
(Post office Regulation.)

IMPORTANT.   Aylesbury.

To finally dispose of - - -
SINGLE DRESS LENGTHS, BLOUSES, CORSETS,
UNDERCLOTHING, SKIRTS, JACKETS,
CHILDREN'S GARMENTS, QUILTS, SHEETS,
BLANKETS, ETC., ETC.,
I intend to hold a Two Days'
SALE 5/= SALE
On FRIDAY @ SATURDAY next,
February 5th and 6th.
REMNANTS AT SPECIAL PRICES.

FRED LONGLEY.

The address to be written here.

Mrs Reeve
Church Farm
Pistone
Tring

97. Another local card used for advertising, this time using the reverse to announce a forthcoming sale by Fred Longley, drapers, in the High Street. The postmark clearly shows the date, 1909. See also card number 70 which shows a detailed view of their window display in 1903. The inscription 'F. LONGLEY'S Drapery Series' shows it to be their own issue, and repeat announcements were probably intended. The pictorial side of the card is shown as number 98 and is of Quarrendon Ruins which were on the outskirts of the town, off the Bicester Road. Judging from the standard of production it would appear to be by one of the well-known publishers of the period.

Quarrendon Ruins, Aylesbury.

98. The other side of number 97 showing the ruins of Quarrendon Church. The 1909 postmark establishes the condition of the church at that time, but it was in fact already in a ruined state back in 1846 when the walls were standing open to the weather as no trace of roofing remained. It had been removed to repair a farmhouse and cottages nearby. The church was probably of early 13th century origin and, at one time, a road ran from here to Bierton, although no trace of it remains today. An appeal was launched in 1848 for restoration before it would be too late to do anything, but nothing came of it and little now remains of the old building.

99. Back to the walking races again (see also card 90) 6th June 1903, the Long Distance Race to Thame and back, finishing at the clock tower. Here we see the start from the Saracen's Head on Rickford's Hill. The race was won by Mr J. Roche who covered the twenty miles in 3 hours 32 minutes. The first prize was one pound. It is interesting to see the varied racing attire.

100. Fêtes were always part of summertime, and in the earlier part of the century quite gala occasions when entertainment was found close to home, and relied solely on local effort. This is the fête held at the Old House, Walton Street 1925. It was organised by Lady Courtown to raise funds to build the Girl Guide's Hall in Beaconsfield Road. G.K. Chesterton was a distinguished visitor.

101. Above: The Aylesbury Railway disaster 23rd December 1904. The Great Central train left Marylebone for Aylesbury with papers, mail and parcels at 2.45 in the morning, Friday 23rd. The crash occurred at 3.40 just outside the station, throwing the engine across the down platform, and wreckage of the carriages all over the permanent way thus completely blocking the station. The Manchester express was approaching the station from the opposite direction at speed. The signalman promptly put the station signal at stop, the Manchester driver slammed on his brakes but it was too late to avoid crashing into the wreckage of the first train, although some reduction in speed lessened the impact and subsequent destruction.

Below: This is another view of the crash. The morning of the disaster was cold and frosty and thick fog. The driver of the Manchester train gave visibility as twenty yards. The noise of the crash brought Mr Roberts, a Metropolitan employee, from Brook Street to help in rescue work, and police sergeant Dance who was on duty in the Market Square also raced down to the station. He said the clock tower was not visible from the top of the square. Doctors Parrott and Baker from Church Street were promptly on the scene and were later joined by Dr Shaw. The London driver, badly scalded and injured, was found where he had been thrown across the down platform. He was quickly removed to the Royal Bucks Hospital. The first body was not extricated until 8 o'clock in the morning, and the second, an hour and a half later.

AYLESBURY RAILWAY DISASTER, DEC 23ᴿᴰ 1904.

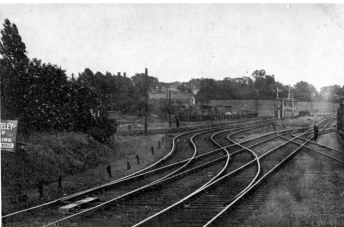

102. Above: All Friday was spent trying to clear wreckage, three steam cranes having been brought in, but it was not until 7 o'clock that evening that the up line was cleared. Passengers from London were having to alight outside the station and walk along the track to the platform. Work continued throughout Friday night by means of light from naphtha torches and bonfires of wreckage from the carriages. The down line was not cleared until 10 o'clock Saturday night. The station was also extensively damaged as much of the wreckage had fallen through the roof.

Below: This is the track just outside the station, the sharp curve of the rails was the main contributing factor of the crash. The driver was not familiar with the run, and not realising he was so near the station, took this bend at too great a speed, throwing the train off the track and tearing up the rails. The first two coaches were completely wrecked. All passengers on both trains were railway employees going on duty. One, who was asleep in the third carriage, was trapped in the wreckage, but the impact of the second train partially freed him and he was rescued, and recovered from his injuries. There were four killed, all on the London train, the driver, fireman and two employees going on duty. The sharp curve was altered soon afterwards.

103. A rare card showing women engine cleaners at the station during the First World War. So great was the shortage of men, that women did many jobs that they had never dreamed of doing before: milk and bread delivery rounds, van and ambulance driving, and of course working in the munition factories. Head bonnets were worn in the factories, not only to keep their hair clean but to prevent the long hair of the day becoming entangled in machinery and the driving belts by which each machine was driven from an overhead shaft.

104. The Aylesbury Royal Mail van in Buckingham Street circa 1904. Note the solid rubber tyres at that period. At least the horn was pneumatic! The hand brake was outside the cab, with fire-fighting appliance alongside. Waterproof curtains protected the driver from wind and rain. The brass headlamps were oil-burning, and easily detached for servicing. The roof rack looks almost like a double-deck with tarpaulin stowed forwards.

105. Another memory of the more recent past. The milkman's float was part of the street scene of the early century. The churn carried the bulk supply of milk, the cans were replenished from the churn. Half pint and pint measures hung from the brass rail on the sides of the can, and would be used to measure the milk required into the jug brought to the door. The cleanliness of the cans and shining brass and condition of the float were the pride of the roundsmen. A ride on the back step to the end of the street gave children more pleasure then than is derived from car outings these days.

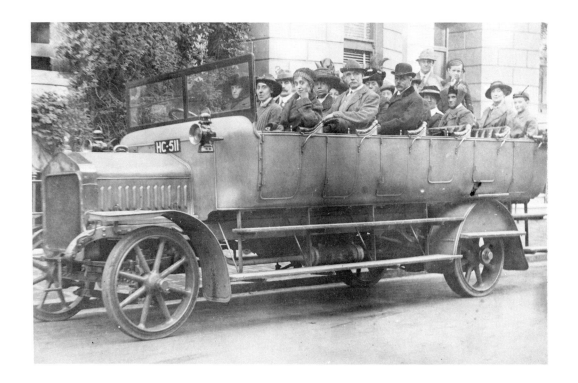

106. Referring to outings, these were typical of the early century — the 'char-a-banc' trips in open, solid-tyred vehicles, usually of short duration, to local places of interest. The 'Silver Queen' was to be found in the Market Square on Sunday afternoons offering trips to Wendover Hills, five miles away, and was soon completely booked up. A very pleasant afternoon out with plenty of time for a walk over the hills to Coombe Hill monument, and back. Char-a-banc parties passing through a town would throw out pennies for children who gathered to watch and cheer as they passed.

COUNCIL SCHOOLS, AYLESBURY

107. The council school, Queen's Park, showing convalescent troops of the First World War in occupation (see card 95). The little local shop kept by the Baldwin sisters, which had been the sweet shop in school days, would be remembered by the soldiers, who had replaced the schoolboy trade. They were good to the wounded men, providing cups of tea and any other comforts they could, extending the normal scope of their shop to the needs of the soldiers.

108. To finish on a lighter note, a 'play pen' circa 1910-1920. Original and efficient, it kept the little lad not only out of harm but out of mischief as well, and gave the poultry a less harassed existence too. It also brings to mind that grocers then received most of their goods in bulk — tea, sugar, rice, soda and many other commodities having to be weighed up for sale. It took a good man to get 112 one pound bags out of a one hundredweight pack. All of Thursday would be spent weighing-up ready for week-end trade. Butter and lard would also be in bulk, needing cutting up, shaping with pats and weighing.